WEALTH UNLEASHED

WEALTH UNLEASHED

Secrets to Building Your Fortune

B. VINCENT

QuillQuest Publishers

CONTENTS

Introduction: Unveiling the Journey to Wealth

Leaving on the Way to Independence from the rat race

The excursion toward independence from the rat race is much the same as setting out on a great journey across unknown waters. It requires planning, assurance, and a guide to direct you to your objective. Similarly as a boat's commander should grasp the ocean, diagram a course, and explore through storms, you too should figure out how to explore the intricacies of individual budget. This way isn't just about arriving at an objective; it's tied in with changing your relationship with cash, producing a way of life that gives pleasure, security, and, at last, opportunity.

Heading out with Objectives

Our endeavor starts with the foundation of clear, feasible monetary objectives. These are the stars by which we explore, directing us through the haziest evenings and the fiercest tempests. Whether it's accomplishing obligation opportunity, claiming a home, getting a familiar retirement, or subsidizing schooling, these objectives should reverberate with your most profound cravings and desires. They are not simply monetary targets; they are the epitome of your fantasies.

Making Your Guide

In view of our objective, we should now graph our course. This includes making an extensive monetary arrangement, a guide that frames the course from where you are presently to where you wish to be. This plan is dynamic, versatile to the changing flows of life. It represents your pay, costs, obligations, and ventures, giving an unmistakable system to designation of assets towards your objectives. Similarly as a guide uncovers the landscape ahead, your monetary arrangement enlightens the means expected to arrive at your monetary goals.

The Breeze in Your Sails: Inspiration and Flexibility

Inspiration is the breeze that drives our boat forward. The power drives us to make a move, to continue through to the end whenever troubles arise. In any case, inspiration can wind down, and the excursion might appear to be overwhelming on occasion. It's at these times that we should remind ourselves why we set out on this journey in any case. Returning to your objectives, praising achievements, and adjusting your arrangement depending on the situation can revive your inspiration, assisting you with remaining lined up with your vision of independence from the rat race.

Exploring Tempests: Conquering Difficulties

No journey is without its tempests. Monetary misfortunes, startling costs, and financial slumps are all important for the excursion. These difficulties test our determination, our flexibility, and our obligation to our objectives. It's critical to expect these obstructions, fabricating a secret stash, and fostering a versatile outlook. Keep in mind, each challenge defeat is an illustration picked up, making us more grounded, savvier, and more able guides of our monetary oceans.

As we set forth on this excursion, recollect that the way to independence from the rat race is interesting for every person. An individual journey mirrors your qualities, needs, and yearnings. With your objectives obviously set, your arrangement solidly close by, and inspiration as your dependable friend, you are exceptional to explore the waters of individual accounting. Allow the experience to start.

Groundworks of Monetary Proficiency

In the mission for independence from the rat race, information is your most important resource. Monetary proficiency, the comprehension of monetary standards and the capacity to utilize this information to go with informed choices, is the foundation whereupon the building of abundance is fabricated. It's similar to learning the language of cash — a language that, once dominated, empowers you to explore the universe of money with certainty and elegance.

The Language of Cash

Envision briefly that cash communicates in its own language. This language, however apparently perplexing, is comprised of crucial ideas like pay, costs, resources, liabilities, and ventures. Similarly as learning another dialect opens up new universes and open doors, understanding the language of cash opens the ways to monetary achievement. It enables you to go with choices that can fundamentally work on your monetary wellbeing and secure your future.

The Mainstays of Monetary Proficiency

The excursion to monetary proficiency starts with dominating four key support points: procuring, saving, effective money management, and spending shrewdly.

Acquiring is tied in with grasping your worth in the commercial center, arranging compensations, and recognizing chances to expand your pay.

Saving includes saving a piece of your pay for sometime later, whether for crises, enormous buys, or growing a substantial financial foundation. It's about discipline, focusing on your monetary future over quick satisfaction.

Contributing is the most common way of utilizing your cash to make more cash. It requires information on various venture vehicles, risk evaluation, and the improvement of an expanded speculation technique that lines up with your monetary objectives.

Spending Carefully involves pursuing informed decisions about your consumptions, recognizing requirements and needs, and keeping away from obligation that doesn't serve your monetary targets.

The Way to Strengthening

As you become conversant in the language of cash, you'll observe that monetary education is something beyond understanding how to spending plan or contribute. About fostering a mentality focuses on monetary wellbeing, perceives open doors for development, and explores difficulties with insight and premonition. This information engages you to assume command over your monetary predetermination, changing dreams of independence from the rat race into reachable real factors.

Ceaseless Learning and Variation

The monetary scene is steadily changing, with new items, advances, and difficulties arising constantly. In this way, monetary proficiency isn't an objective however an excursion of persistent learning and variation. It includes remaining informed about monetary patterns, administrative changes, and new monetary devices. By focusing on long lasting learning, you guarantee that your monetary information stays important and strong, fit for directing you through the intricacies of the monetary world.

Leaving on the way to monetary proficiency is perhaps of the most compensating venture you can make in yourself. It establishes the groundwork for a fate of independence from the rat race, security, and thriving. With every idea dominated, you draw one stage nearer to opening the insider facts of abundance and releasing your monetary potential.

Motivation from Examples of overcoming adversity

At the core of each and every extraordinary accomplishment lies an account of assurance, strength, and win. As we venture through the scenes of monetary proficiency and establishing a strong financial foundation, the stories of those have explored the way before us that enlighten our direction. These stories act as signals of motivation as well as pragmatic aides, offering bits of knowledge into the procedures and outlooks that can drive us toward our monetary objectives.

The Force of Genuine Models

In a world overflowing with hypothetical information and dynamic ideas, the tales of genuine people who have made monetary progress ground us truly. They show that independence from the rat race is achievable, for the astoundingly gifted or fortunate, yet for anybody ready to focus on the excursion. From the business person who began with only a fantasy and a persistent hard working attitude, to the representative who boosted their reserve funds and speculations to resign early, these accounts are a demonstration of the force of constancy, vital preparation, and monetary proficiency.

Different Ways to Progress

What makes these examples of overcoming adversity so convincing is their variety. They advise us that there is nobody size-fits-all way to deal with creating financial wellbeing. While one individual might track down fortune in the financial exchange, another may fabricate a land domain or send off a notable startup. These differed ways highlight the significance of fitting your establishing long term financial stability technique to your special abilities, interests, and conditions. They urge you to think imaginatively, to investigate whimsical open doors, and to make an excursion that resounds with your own vision of progress.

Illustrations Learned and Techniques Shared

Past motivation, these examples of overcoming adversity are rich with useful insight. They offer an in the background take a gander at the systems that have demonstrated compelling in exploring the monetary scene. From definite planning methods and smart speculation decisions to inventive revenue sources and successful gamble the executives, the examples gathered from these accounts are priceless. They give a guide, featuring possible entanglements to stay away from and best practices to copy.

The Human Component of Monetary Achievement

Maybe above all, these accounts refine the course of growing a strong financial foundation. They uncover the apprehensions, difficulties, and misfortunes that frequently go with the excursion, advising us that monetary achievement isn't just about numbers and graphs, yet about the genuine, lived encounters of people. These stories cultivate a feeling of association and compassion, empowering us to endure through our own monetary difficulties and to help others in their journeys for independence from the rat race.

As you leave on your own excursion toward riches and thriving, let these accounts of accomplishment rouse you. Permit them to act as a wake up call that your objectives are feasible, that snags can be survived, and that the way to independence from the rat race is as much about the excursion for all intents and purposes about the objective. With every part of your own story that you compose, recollect that you are pursuing your own monetary accomplishment as well as making ready for others to emulate your example.

Chapter 1: The Foundation of Wealth Building

Planning for Progress

The foundation of creating a post of financial stability lies not in that frame of mind of our desires, but rather in the ordinary, regular choices we bring in about our cash. Planning, frequently neglected in its effortlessness, is the establishment whereupon domains of abundance are assembled. The signal aides us through the obscurity of monetary vulnerability, enlightening the way to independence from the rat race.

The Quintessence of Planning

At its center, planning is an arrangement for your cash. A deliberate methodology includes following your pay, grasping your costs, and arriving at cognizant conclusions about how to dispense your assets. It's tied in with assuming command over your monetary fate, each dollar in turn. Similarly as a designer needs a plan to construct a construction that endures over the extreme long haul, you want a financial plan to fabricate a monetary future that is secure, prosperous, and versatile.

Making Your Monetary Diagram

The method involved with making a spending plan is both a craftsmanship and a science. It begins with a nitty gritty stock of your month to month pay, trailed by an exhaustive investigation of your spending. This incorporates fixed costs, like lease and utilities, and variable costs, similar to food and amusement. The objective isn't to limit your bliss however to guarantee that your spending lines up with your qualities and needs.

The Essential Allotment of Assets

With a reasonable comprehension of your monetary scene, you can start to decisively designate assets more. This implies focusing on fundamental costs, distinguishing regions where you can scale back, and concluding the amount you can save and contribute towards your future objectives. The sorcery of planning lies in its capacity to change your monetary objectives from far off dreams into feasible real factors.

Changing the Sails

A spending plan is definitely not a set-and-neglect report; it's a no nonsense arrangement that requires customary survey and change. Life is dynamic — your pay might vacillate, your objectives might advance, and unforeseen costs will emerge. The way to fruitful planning is adaptability. By consistently looking into your spending plan, you can change your spending, saving, and growth strategies to keep on track toward your monetary targets.

The Force of Cognizant Spending

At last, planning enables you to settle on cognizant spending choices. It shows you the worth of cash, showing you how little, careful changes in your ways of managing money can prompt critical monetary development after some time. About pursuing informed decisions mirror your objectives, values, and desires.

In the stupendous embroidery of establishing long term financial stability, planning is the string that winds around together your fantasies and your activities. It is an act of care and discipline that, when dominated, can open ways to overflow and flourishing. By committing yourself to the standards of planning for progress, you establish the groundwork for a future where independence from the rat race isn't simply a chance, however a sureness.

Crisis Assets and Monetary Security

In the ensemble of establishing financial stability, in the event that planning is the beat, the rainy day account is the concordance that carries equilibrium and strength to your monetary creation. It's a monetary support intended to defend against the unanticipated tempests of life, guaranteeing that when confronted with startling costs or monetary slumps, your way to abundance stays unshaken.

The Wellbeing Net Standard

A backup stash goes about as a wellbeing net, ready to get you in the midst of monetary trouble. Whether it's an unexpected employment cutback, a health related crisis, or critical home fixes, life's eccentricism requests readiness. This asset guarantees that such amazements don't crash your drawn out monetary objectives or power you into obligation. It's tied in with enjoying the harmony of psyche to zero in on arrangements as opposed to agonizing over monetary aftermath.

Working out Your Pad

Deciding the size of your backup stash is a critical stage in this cycle. The standard way of thinking recommends saving between three to a half year of everyday costs. This estimation depends on your month to month expenses, considering your way of life, commitments, and the soundness of your pay. The objective is to make a cushion sufficiently significant to cover your requirements during surprising monetary difficulties without being extreme.

Building Your Asset

The excursion to laying out a completely subsidized crisis hold is gradual. It begins with setting a primer objective, maybe $1,000, and afterward deliberately saving towards it. This could include dispensing a part of your month to month financial plan or directing bonuses, similar to government forms or rewards, into your backup stash. The key is consistency and prioritization, regarding this asset as a non-debatable part of your monetary arrangement.

Where to Keep Your Rainy day account

Openness and conservation of significant worth are vital while picking where to stash your rainy day account. High return investment accounts, currency market records, or transient authentications of store are well known decisions. These choices offer liquidity, permitting you to pull out assets without huge punishments or postponements, while likewise giving an unassuming profit from your reserve funds.

The Mental and Monetary Effect

The genuine worth of a backup stash reaches out past the money related. It's a demonstration of your monetary discipline and a foundation of your inner harmony. Realizing you have a monetary pad sets you up for the startling as well as imparts a feeling of safety that saturates all parts of your life. It empowers you to settle on choices from a position of solidarity as opposed to franticness, keeping you immovable on your way to riches.

Generally, a backup stash isn't simply a monetary methodology; it's an interest in your prosperity and a basic component of a strong establishing long term financial stability establishment. By devoting yourself to the creation and support of this asset, you weave a well-being net that safeguards your fantasies, guaranteeing that regardless of what life tosses your direction, your excursion toward independence from the rat race proceeds unabated.

Obligation The board and Disposal

In the scene of monetary prosperity, obligation frequently lingers like a shadow, fit for darkening the way to riches. However, when drawn nearer with intelligence and system, the test of obligation changes from a hindrance into an achievement on the excursion to independence from the rat race. Overseeing and eventually taking out obligation isn't just about numbers; it's a significant demonstration of recovering command over your monetary future.

The Idea of Obligation

Obligation, in its embodiment, is acquired future. It's a promise to take care of cash that has been loaned to you, frequently with premium. While some obligation can act as a switch, pushing you toward objectives like homeownership or schooling, different structures can capture you in a pattern of installments that impede abundance collection. Recognizing 'great' obligation, which can possibly build your total assets or create pay, and 'awful' obligation, which doesn't, is the most vital phase in dominating your monetary predetermination.

Methodologies for Decrease

The excursion to obligation opportunity starts with a thorough evaluation of your commitments. Posting every one of your obligations, from the littlest Visa equilibrium to the biggest home loan, gives clearness and viewpoint. The famous "snowball" strategy proposes zeroing in on taking care of the littlest obligations first, steadily moving gradually up to the bigger ones, in this way picking up speed and inspiration. On the other hand, the "torrential slide" strategy focuses on obligations with the most elevated loan costs, getting a good deal on interest installments over the long haul.

Discussion and Solidification

In exploring obligation, openness is of the utmost importance. Numerous leasers will arrange terms, whether through financing cost decreases, installment deferrals, or rebuilding plans. For those shuffling different obligations, union into a solitary credit with a lower loan fee can improve on installments and speed up the way to obligation opportunity. In any case, this approach expects discipline to abstain from collecting new obligation, transforming a momentary help into a drawn out triumph.

The Mental Fight

Past the strategic moves under water the board lies a mental fight. Obligation frequently conveys close to home weight, appearing as pressure, uneasiness, or disgrace. Beating this requires something other than monetary keenness; it requests flexibility, persistence, and a change in context. Seeing every installment not as a misfortune but rather as a stage toward freedom can change the excursion into an enabling encounter.

Making an Obligation Free Future

The disposal of obligation denotes a critical second in establishing financial stability, opening up assets that can be diverted toward reserve funds, speculations, and different vehicles of development. It's a resurrection of sorts, offering a fresh start whereupon to construct a future unrestricted by past commitments.

Obligation the board and disposal is a basic part in the story of monetary freedom. It's a demonstration of the influence of procedure, discipline, and diligence in conquering difficulties and opening the ways to riches. By embracing this excursion, you not just prepare for a more brilliant monetary future yet additionally for a day to day existence wealthy in conceivable outcomes and liberated from the chains of obligation.

Putting resources into Yourself

At the center of each and every establishing long term financial stability venture lies a central truth: the most powerful and persevering through resource you have is yourself. Putting resources into self-awareness, training, and expertise procurement isn't just a demonstration of personal development yet an essential move in the terrific round of monetary thriving. This section unfurls the outline for tackling the endless potential inside, changing it into a reference point that guides you toward unmatched riches and achievement.

The Underpinning of Self-Venture

Putting resources into yourself rises above the ordinary monetary insight of stocks, bonds, and land. It is tied in with perceiving that your capacities, information, and abilities are the bedrock where-upon abundance is fabricated. This speculation appears in different structures — constant learning, wellbeing and health, systems ad-ministration, and self-awareness. Every one of these areas adds to upgrading your worth in the commercial center, hoisting your true capacity for procuring and, accordingly, your ability for abundance creation.

Schooling and Ability Procurement

The quest for information and abilities is the most immediate type of self-speculation. In a steadily developing financial scene, remaining applicable means remaining taught. This could be formal schooling, like degrees and confirmations, or casual learning through internet based courses, studios, and books. The goal is to develop a range of abilities that expands your employability and procuring potential as well as prepares you to explore the intricacies of the monetary world with keenness and certainty.

Wellbeing and Health: The Abundance Association

Frequently ignored in conversations of monetary success, physi-cal and mental prosperity are basic parts of supportable growing a substantial financial foundation. Wellbeing is a type of abundance in itself, empowering you to seek after your objectives with energy and strength. Besides, wellbeing rehearses lessen medical care costs over the long haul, protect your procuring limit, and improve your general personal satisfaction. Putting resources into your wellbeing is a significant assertion of dignity and a central component of long haul monetary system.

Organizing: Creating Financial wellbeing Through Connections

The maxim "It's not what you know, however who you know" highlights the benefit of systems administration in abundance creation. Building a different and steady organization opens ways to potential open doors, information, and assets that could somehow stay unavailable. Concentrating intently on developing significant expert connections can speed up your profession direction, give mentorship open doors, and acquaint you with speculation and undertakings. Organizing is an interest in the social capital that can yield profits far surpassing beginning assumptions.

The Far reaching influence of Self-improvement

Putting resources into yourself sets off a far reaching influence that stretches out past your nearby monetary profits. It encourages a mentality of development, flexibility, and versatility — characteristics fundamental for exploring the vulnerabilities of life and money. This outlook pushes you toward independence from the rat race as well as enhances your existence with a feeling of direction and satisfaction.

All in all, the quintessence of establishing a strong financial foundation lies not in the outside procurement of resources but rather in the interior development of one's capacities. By committing assets to self-improvement, instruction, health, and systems administration, you upgrade your monetary possibilities as well as leave on an excursion of change that rises above the material. Putting resources into yourself is a definitive articulation of confidence in your true capacity, a responsibility that prepares for an eventual fate of overflow, flourishing, and achievement.

Chapter 2: Investing Basics

Grasping the Financial exchange

The financial exchange remains as a reference point of chance, a lively biological system where people and foundations join to put resources into the motors of business and development. At its center, the securities exchange isn't simply about trading shares; it is tied in with taking part in the development and flourishing of organizations around the world. This section demystifies the securities exchange, directing you through its complexities and uncovering how it can act as a strong vehicle for abundance creation.

The Substance of Stocks

A stock addresses an offer in the responsibility for organization. At the point when you buy a stock, you become a section proprietor of that organization, despite how little your portion might be. This proprietorship qualifies you for a piece of the organization's benefits, frequently delivered out as profits, and awards you a stake in its future. The appeal of the securities exchange lies in this immediate connection between your monetary fortunes and the progress of the organizations in which you contribute.

The Commercial center

The securities exchange works through trades, for example, the New York Stock Trade (NYSE) and the Nasdaq, where stocks are traded. These trades act as the heartbeat of the monetary world, throbbing with the cadence of market interest. Costs vary in light of a horde of elements, including organization execution, monetary pointers, and market feeling. Understanding these elements is vital to exploring the market's back and forth movements.

Venture Vehicles

Inside the domain of the financial exchange, financial backers approach an assortment of speculation vehicles, each with its own qualities and systems.

Individual Stocks permit financial backers to buy partakes in unambiguous organizations, offering an immediate method for taking part in their development or decline.

Bonds address credits made by financial backers to enterprises or legislatures, giving a constant flow of pay through interest installments.

Shared Assets and Trade Exchanged Assets (ETFs) empower financial backers to pool their cash to purchase a differentiated arrangement of stocks, securities, or different resources, oversaw by proficient asset chiefs.

Every one of these choices conveys its own harmony between hazard and possible award, and the decision among them ought to be educated by your monetary objectives, risk resilience, and venture skyline.

The Gamble Award Worldview

Putting resources into the securities exchange is intrinsically unsafe, however it likewise offers the potential for critical prizes. The way to effective financial planning isn't to take out risk however to comprehend and oversee it. Differentiating your ventures, leading careful exploration, and keeping a drawn out point of view are significant systems for relieving risk while situating yourself to benefit from the development capability of the market.

The Way to Abundance

For those ready to become familiar with its language and regard its powers, the securities exchange offers a way to monetary freedom. It requests discipline, persistence, and a steady obligation to persistent learning. As you set out on this excursion, let this part act as your compass, directing you through the intricacies of the securities exchange and enlightening the way toward creating and supporting financial stability.

Land Financial planning

Wandering into the domain of land financial planning is likened to investigating a tremendous, unique scene, rich with open doors for both development and challenge. This part digs into the fundamental components of land as a speculation procedure, unwinding the intricacies and divulging the potential it holds for creating significant financial wellbeing. Land effective money management, with its unmistakable resources and potential for both automated revenue and capital appreciation, offers an exceptional mix of security and development that is unequaled in the speculation world.

The Groundworks of Land Venture

Land speculation rises above the straightforward acquisition of property. An essential undertaking includes the obtaining, the board, and deal or rental of property for benefit. Dissimilar to stocks or bonds, land is an actual resource, offering financial backers a feeling of substance and control. This area is portrayed by its variety, enveloping private properties, business land, modern spaces, and land.

Techniques for Progress

Progress in land requests something beyond capital; it requires knowledge, tirelessness, and flexibility. Key techniques include:

Investment properties: Buying property to lease to occupants, giving a constant flow of recurring, automated revenue while the actual property values in esteem.

House Flipping: The specialty of purchasing properties needing fix, remodeling them, and selling them for a benefit.

Land Venture Trusts (REITs): Putting resources into land through organizations that own, work, or money pay delivering land, offering a method for putting resources into land without possessing actual property.

Exploring the Market

Understanding business sector patterns, financial pointers, and neighborhood factors is critical in land. Area, market interest, loan costs, and financial cycles all assume critical parts in deciding the outcome of land speculations. Adroit financial backers figure out how to peruse these signs, adjusting their techniques to exploit economic situations and relieve gambles.

Functional Contemplations

Land money management isn't without its difficulties. It includes contemplations like property the board, support, occupant relations, and administrative consistence. Moreover, the somewhat illiquid nature of land requires a drawn out viewpoint, as properties won't be easily sold without possibly causing misfortunes.

The Way to Abundance Through Land

Putting resources into land offers a convincing way to riches, joining the potential for recurring, automated revenue with the enthusiasm for resource esteem. It requires a mix of vital preparation, market information, and functional clever. For those able to explore its intricacies, land effective money management can give monetary awards as well as the fulfillment of building something persevering.

As we investigate the complexities of land putting resources into this part, recall that the excursion is as much about the examples advanced en route for what it's worth about the objective. Land isn't simply an interest in property yet an interest in your future, offering an unmistakable heritage that can persevere for ages.

Elective Ventures

Past the natural domains of stocks and land lies a less customary scene, a domain of different and frequently charming venture open doors known as elective speculations. This part leaves on an investigation of these flighty resources, revealing insight into their special qualities, expected benefits, and inborn dangers. Elective ventures incorporate a wide cluster of resources, including products, digital currencies, and confidential value, each offering unmistakable pathways to abundance past conventional business sectors.

Investigating the Flighty

Elective ventures challenge simple order, crossing an expansive range from substantial resources like craftsmanship and wine to monetary instruments, for example, flexible investments and subordinates. Their appeal lies in their true capacity for exceptional yields as well as in their ability to broaden speculation portfolios, diminishing generally risk through low relationship with customary business sectors.

Items: Putting resources into natural substances like gold, oil, and farming items can offer a fence against expansion and cash debasement.

Cryptographic forms of money: Computerized monetary standards and blockchain innovations address a state of the art boondocks, offering outstanding learning experiences close by critical unpredictability.

Confidential Value: Putting resources into privately owned businesses offers the opportunity to be important for possibly high-development ventures before they open up to the world, yet with higher dangers and longer speculation skylines.

The Enhancement Benefit

One of the vital benefits of elective ventures is enhancement. By consolidating resources that act uniquely in contrast to stocks and securities, financial backers can make a stronger portfolio equipped for enduring business sector variances. This expansion can upgrade returns while moderating gamble, a rule that lies at the core of sound speculation system.

Exploring Dangers

Nonetheless, the way through elective speculations is laden with difficulties. These resources frequently accompany higher expenses, restricted liquidity, and less straightforwardness than customary ventures, requiring intensive expected level of effort and a sharp comprehension of the particular market elements at play. Also, the high-reward capability of elective speculations is perpetually connected to higher dangers, including market unpredictability, administrative changes, and mechanical vulnerabilities on account of digital currencies.

Key Reconciliation into Your Portfolio

Integrating elective interests into your portfolio requests an essential methodology. It includes adjusting the craving for better yields with the requirement for risk the executives, adjusting your speculation decisions to your monetary objectives, risk resistance, and venture skyline. For some financial backers, elective resources comprise a little yet imperative part of a balanced speculation system, offering both the excitement of revelation and the potential for huge monetary prizes.

Leaving on the Elective Way

This section welcomes you to consider the extensive universe of elective speculations as a feature of your growing a substantial financial foundation venture. While exploring this space requires alert, a bold soul, and a craving for learning, the prizes can be significant. Elective speculations offer the potential for monetary development as well as advance your financial planning experience, furnishing chances to draw in with arising patterns and developments molding the fate of money.

As we dive further into the complexities of elective speculations, recall that this excursion isn't for the cowardly. It is a way for the inquisitive, the visionary, and the tireless — an undertaking that widens your venture skyline and moves you to think past the traditional, opening new elements of abundance creation.

Risk The board

In the great embroidery of venture, chance and award are inseparably woven together, each string reliant upon the other, molding the examples of abundance that arise over the long haul. This section digs into the basic craftsmanship and study of chance administration, a discipline that guarantees the quest for monetary development doesn't prompt ruin yet rather to a manageable and prosperous future. Understanding, surveying, and decisively overseeing risk isn't simply a piece of financial planning — it is the very substance that isolates the effective from the speculative.

The Idea of Speculation Hazard

Risk, in its least complex structure, is the chance of losing some or the entirety of a speculation. However, additionally the impetus drives possible returns. Various sorts of ventures convey various degrees of chance, impacted by elements like market instability, financial cycles, international occasions, and individual organization execution. The most vital phase in risk the board is perceiving that chance can't be disposed of; it must be perceived and alleviated.

Systems for Relieving Hazard

Moderating gamble includes a complex methodology that incorporates:

Broadening: Spreading speculations across different resource classes, businesses, and geographic areas to diminish openness to any single wellspring of chance.

Resource Allotment: Fitting the blend of venture types to line up with a singular's gamble resistance, speculation skyline, and monetary objectives. This essential conveyance goes about as a cradle against market unpredictability.

Customary Rebalancing: Changing the speculation portfolio occasionally to keep up with the ideal degree of hazard, particularly as market developments might move the underlying equilibrium.

Figuring out Chance Resilience: Surveying one's solace with risk, both monetarily and inwardly, to guarantee that speculation choices line up with individual inclinations and rest soundly around evening time levels.

The Job of Hazard in Venture Procedure

The administration of hazard isn't just about aversion yet about enhancement. It's tied in with finding the right harmony among chance and return that matches your monetary objectives and time period. This equilibrium is dynamic, developing as your life conditions, monetary goals, and economic situations change. An effectively thought out risk the executives technique embraces this ease, giving a structure to pursuing informed choices that improve the potential for abundance gathering while at the same time safeguarding against pointless misfortunes.

Embracing Chance as a Way to Development

A long way from being a hindrance, risk is a pathway to development. It moves financial backers to be educated, to remain drew in with their speculations, and to contemplate what's to come. By overseeing risk really, you can take advantage of chances that others might neglect, transforming vulnerability into a wellspring of potential.

The Persevering through Worth of Hazard The board

This section highlights the persevering through worth of hazard the board as a basic part of the speculation cycle. A discipline requires watchfulness, discipline, and a pledge to consistent learning. As you explore the intricacies of effective financial planning, let the standards of hazard the executives be your aide, enlightening the way toward monetary achievement and dependability. Keep in mind, in the domain of effective money management, chance and prize are accomplices in the dance of abundance creation; dominating their developments is the way to accomplishing your monetary goals.

Chapter 3: Advanced Wealth Building Strategies

Utilizing Build Interest

In the domain of cutting edge establishing financial stability methodologies, the influence of self multiplying dividends remains as a demonstration of the class of science in making riches. Frequently hailed as the eighth miracle of the world, build revenue is the motor that moves little interests into tremendous fortunes after some time. This part discloses the enchanted behind accumulate interest and guides you through outfitting speeding up your excursion to monetary independence potential.

The Wizardry of Accruing funds

At its center, build revenue is revenue acquired on interest. It is the cycle by which an amount of cash develops dramatically over the long haul, as the profit on an underlying speculation produce their own income thus. This peculiarity happens when the premium acquired on your speculations is reinvested, as opposed to taken out, permitting your abundance to accelerate over the natural course of time.

The Standard of 72

A basic method for getting a handle on the force of self multiplying dividends is through the Standard of 72, a speedy recipe to gauge what amount of time it will require for a venture to twofold given a proper yearly pace of interest. By separating 72 by the yearly pace of return, you can get a good guess of the quantity of years it will take for your underlying venture to become twofold. This standard highlights the significance of both the pace of return and time in expanding the effect of accumulating funds.

Procedures for Augmenting Build Interest

Boosting the advantages of self multiplying dividends includes something other than grasping its standards; it requires vital activity:

Begin Early: The sooner you begin financial planning, the additional time your cash needs to compound, accentuating the significant effect of time on your speculation development.

Contribute Routinely: Steady speculations after some time, even in modest quantities, can prompt huge abundance collection on account of accumulated dividends.

Reinvest Profit: Naturally reinvesting profits and premium installments accumulates the development of your speculations.

Pick the Right Speculation Vehicles: Exorbitant premium bank accounts, stocks, shared reserves, and different ventures that offer higher paces of return can essentially upgrade the force of building.

The Way to Abundance Through Accumulate Interest

The excursion to abundance through build interest is both a long distance race and a run. It rewards tolerance and discipline, as the main development happens in the later stages. By settling on informed choices, contributing shrewdly, and permitting time to do something amazing, you can open the maximum capacity of accumulated dividends. This methodology enables you to fabricate a significant monetary establishment, transforming the fantasy of independence from the rat race into an unmistakable reality.

Embrace the discipline of customary, long haul effective financial planning, and let build interest outline your course to riches. As you proceed to contribute and reinvest, you'll observer the change of your monetary scene, where every dollar works indefatigably for your benefit, preparing to a fate of overflow and security.

Charge Procedures for Abundance Boost

In the many-sided dance of growing a strong financial foundation, excelling at charge system assumes a basic part in upgrading the tune of your monetary development. Charges, while a conviction in the monetary scene, offer open doors for canny financial backers to explore their commitments in a manner that expands riches. This part digs into the nuanced universe of assessment systems, enlightening ways through the financial labyrinth that lead to significant reserve funds and, thusly, more noteworthy abundance gathering.

The Significance of Assessment Effective Money management

Understanding the effect of charges on your speculations is central. Every venture vehicle accompanies its own assessment suggestions, impacting the net profit from your speculations. Charge effective financial planning includes choosing ventures and records that limit charge responsibility, subsequently boosting your after-assessment forms. It's tied in with knowing where to put your resources for make the most of tax breaks and keep away from superfluous taxation rates.

Charge Advantaged Records

One of the cornerstones of expense system is the usage of duty advantaged records like IRAs, 401(k)s, and HSAs. These records offer critical tax cuts, including charge conceded development or tax-exempt withdrawals, making them amazing assets in the abundance developer's munititions stockpile. By getting it and decisively adding to these records, you can decrease your available pay, concede charges, and now and again, pull out reserves tax-exempt in retirement.

Grasping Capital Additions

Exploring the waters of capital increases charge is one more imperative part of duty proficient financial planning. Long haul capital increases, acknowledged on ventures held for over a year, are charged at a lower rate than momentary additions. Decisively arranging the offer of resources for fit the bill for long haul capital additions charge rates can fundamentally decrease your expense responsibility, permitting a greater amount of your speculation gets back to intensify after some time.

Collecting Misfortunes to Counterbalance Gains

Charge misfortune gathering is a modern technique that includes getting rid of interests in an inopportune time to balance capital additions charges on different speculations. This strategy lessens your expense responsibility as well as permits you to reinvest the returns into additional promising open doors, keeping up with the energy of your speculation development.

The Cooperative energy of Arranging and Expert Counsel

Compelling duty arranging is a continuous cycle, requiring steady cautiousness and variation to changing regulations and individual conditions. Working with charge experts and monetary guides can give significant bits of knowledge, assisting you with fitting your venture procedures to your extraordinary circumstance while remaining agreeable with charge regulations.

Hoisting Your Abundance through Expense Procedure

Charge techniques for abundance expansion are about something other than setting aside cash; they're tied in with upgrading the development of your interests in an expense effective way. By embracing these methodologies, you change charges from an impressive obstruction into a sensible component of your monetary arrangement. As you explore the intricacies of the duty scene, let this section act as your aide, enabling you to settle on informed choices that upgrade your riches and secure your monetary future.

Building Recurring sources of income

The mission for independence from the rat race is an excursion toward making a daily existence where your time isn't exclusively traded for cash, however where your resources work for you, producing pay even as you rest. This section investigates the groundbreaking influence of automated revenue — a basic point of support in the design of growing a substantial financial foundation. Automated sources of income, by their tendency, offer the charm of monetary security with less immediate time speculation, giving a consistent progression of pay that can uphold your way of life and speed up your growing long term financial stability tries.

The Quintessence of Recurring, automated revenue

Automated revenue is characterized as profit got from an undertaking wherein the financial backer isn't effectively elaborate consistently. Not at all like dynamic pay, which is procured from playing out a help, recurring, automated revenue is created from speculations, organizations, or resources that require a forthright venture and insignificant continuous work to keep up with. The way to opening this stream lies in the underlying work to make or put resources into sources that keep on producing income over the long run.

Techniques for Creating Recurring, automated revenue

A few roads exist for building automated revenue, each with its own arrangement of advantages and contemplations:

Profit Effective financial planning: Putting resources into profit paying stocks or assets can give a normal, unsurprising stream of pay. The key is to put resources into stable organizations with a solid history of delivering profits.

Rental Pay: Land keeps on being a leaned toward course for recurring, automated revenue. Whether through long haul rentals or transient excursion rentals, possessing property can turn out reliable month to month revenue as well as appreciation in esteem after some time.

Making Computerized Items: In the advanced age, making and selling computerized items — like digital books, courses, or programming — offers a versatile method for creating pay. When made, these items can be sold over and over without extra creation costs.

Subsidiary Showcasing: By advancing others' items or administrations, you can acquire commissions from deals made through your reference. This methodology tackles the force of your organization or online presence to latently produce pay.

The Intensifying Impact of Recurring, automated revenue

The genuine influence of recurring, automated revenue lies in its capability to compound and speed up growing long term financial stability. By reinvesting the profit from automated revenue sources, you can dramatically expand your abundance after some time. Besides, recurring, automated revenue gives a pad of monetary security, decreasing dependence on dynamic pay and offering more opportunity to seek after different interests or ventures.

Difficulties and Contemplations

While automated revenue offers various benefits, it's essential to recognize the difficulties and contemplations included. Introductory speculations, whether of time, cash, or both, are frequently significant. Moreover, overseeing and keeping up with pay sources, especially in land, can require exertion and assets. Nonetheless, with legitimate preparation, exploration, and the board, these difficulties can be explored effectively.

Opening Independence from the rat race

Building recurring sources of income is an undertaking that embodies the guideline of thinking about the big picture before attacking the details. About making key ventures deliver profits as time, opportunity, and monetary development. As this part unfurls, recollect that the excursion to making recurring, automated revenue is one of persistence, steadiness, and vital activity. By differentiating your revenue sources and putting resources into resources that create continuous returns, you make ready toward accomplishing genuine monetary autonomy and opening the abundance that lies past the limitations of time and work.

Business venture and Business Possession

The quest for abundance frequently prompts the prolific grounds of business venture and business possession, where visionaries and visionaries try to change their thoughts into unmistakable real factors. This part wanders into the core of abundance creation from the perspective of business venture, featuring the unmatched open doors it presents for building significant, enduring riches. Here, we investigate the quintessence of enterprising achievement, the essential moves that raise a business from commencement to thriving, and the significant effect of possession on your monetary scene.

The Enterprising Soul: Groundwork of Riches

Business venture is more than the demonstration of beginning a business; it's a mentality — a persistent quest for development, critical thinking, and worth creation. Business visionaries are the designers of their monetary fates, utilizing their interests, abilities, and assurance to assemble endeavors that produce pay as well as make an incentive for their networks and society at large. This excursion, while loaded with dangers and difficulties, offers the potential for outstanding development and individual satisfaction past the bounds of conventional business.

Building Blocks of Effective Business Possession

The way to fruitful business possession is cleared with key preparation, market understanding, and monetary discernment. Key components include:

Distinguishing Business sector Needs: Fruitful organizations are in many cases brought into the world from a profound comprehension of market holes or neglected needs. Business visionaries who acutely notice market drifts and pay attention to client criticism are better situated to offer arrangements that reverberate with their interest group.

Vital Preparation and Execution: Changing a thought into a beneficial business requires careful preparation, setting clear targets, and executing systems with accuracy. This incorporates fostering a strong plan of action, showcasing plan, and functional system to guarantee the business can scale and adjust as it develops.

Monetary Administration: Authority over the business' monetary wellbeing is essential. This includes overseeing income, getting subsidizing, and going with informed venture choices that guarantee the business' drawn out manageability and development.

Utilizing Innovation: In the present computerized age, innovation assumes a vital part in business proficiency and versatility. Business visionaries who embrace mechanical arrangements can smooth out activities, contact more extensive crowds, and make upper hands in their enterprises.

The Abundance Capability of Business Possession

A definitive prize of business venture and business proprietorship lies in producing huge wealth potential. In addition to the fact that effective organizations give a constant stream of pay, yet they likewise fabricate resources that value over the long haul. Besides, entrepreneurs have the special chance to influence their enterprises, enhance, and add to monetary development, all while building an inheritance that rises above monetary achievement.

Exploring the Enterprising Scene

Leaving on an enterprising endeavor is an excursion set apart by ups and downs, triumphs and disappointments. It requests strength, flexibility, and a readiness to gain from each insight. Business visionaries should be ready to confront vulnerability, settle on hard decisions, and, when fundamental, turn their systems in light of market elements.

Determination: Business as a Way to Riches

Business venture and business proprietorship address one of the most difficult yet compensating ways to abundance creation. An excursion calls for boldness, vision, and an enduring obligation to greatness. As this section finishes up, let it act as both an aide and a motivation for the individuals who decide to set out on the innovative way. The way to abundance through business proprietorship isn't for the cowardly, yet for the individuals who continue, it offers the commitment of independence from the rat race, individual fulfillment, and the potential chance to make history.

Chapter 4: Wealth Protection and Estate Planning

Protection and Abundance Security

In the fabulous methodology of abundance creation, the significance of protection is in many cases eclipsed by the appeal of gathering. However, the protection of abundance through protection is a principal mainstay of a sound monetary arrangement. This section dives into the basic job of different kinds of protection in shielding the abundance you've worked resolutely to fabricate. It's tied in with making a rampart against the unanticipated, guaranteeing that your monetary establishment stays in salvageable shape despite life's vulnerabilities.

The Embodiment of Protection

Protection, in its different structures, goes about as a monetary wellbeing net, giving security and genuine serenity. By moving the monetary gamble of specific misfortunes to an insurance agency, you safeguard yourself, your family, and your resources from unexpected occasions that could have wrecking monetary ramifications.

Whether it's an unexpected sickness, a mishap, property harm, or some other surprising event, having the right protection inclusion can mean the contrast between a brief difficulty and a monetary disaster.

Kinds of Protection for Abundance Insurance

Life coverage: Fills in as a foundation of abundance assurance, offering monetary security to your friends and family in case of your troublesome passing. It can assist with covering remarkable obligations, accommodate your family's future necessities, and guarantee that your bequest plan is executed as expected.

Health care coverage: Prepares for the significant expenses of clinical consideration, shielding your abundance from being dissolved by clinic bills, physician recommended drugs, and other wellbeing related costs. In a scene where medical services costs keep on rising, health care coverage is key.

Property Protection: Safeguards your actual resources — your home, vehicle, and individual property — from harm or misfortune because of burglary, fire, cataclysmic events, and different risks. It's tied in with defending the worth of your resources as well as your capacity to recuperate and remake.

Responsibility Protection: Safeguards you from monetary misfortune if you're seen as lawfully answerable for making injury someone else or harming their property. It's a frequently ignored part of abundance insurance, yet it's essential for moderating the gamble of claims that could risk your monetary solidness.

Assessing Your Protection Needs

The most common way of deciding the right sort and measure of protection inclusion is exceptionally private and relies upon different variables, including what is going on, family construction, resources, and chance resistance. Normal audits of your insurance contracts are fundamental to guarantee that your inclusion advances with your evolving needs, offering ideal security as you explore through various phases of life.

The Essential Job of Protection in Abundance The executives

Protection isn't simply a cost; it's an essential interest in your family's security and your monetary genuine serenity. By sensibly choosing the suitable insurance contracts, you make a defensive channel around your riches, defending the your rewards for so much hard work against unforeseen occasions. This part highlights the fundamental job of protection in a complete abundance the executives system, featuring its significance in safeguarding riches, yet additionally in giving a tradition of monetary security for those you care about the most.

In the design of your monetary future, let protection be the bedrock on which you fabricate a tradition of getting through solidness and security.

Home Arranging Fundamentals

As the story of your life unfurls, the inheritance you decide to leave behind turns into a necessary part. Bequest arranging, frequently saw as a mind boggling and grave errand, is on a very basic level a demonstration of clearness and liberality towards those you hold dear. It's tied in with guaranteeing that your abundance, gathered through long stretches of persistence and key prescience, is conveyed by your desires, getting your heritage and accommodating your friends and family. This part directs you through the basic parts of bequest arranging, enlightening its importance in the abundance the executives adventure.

The Embodiment of Home Preparation

Domain arranging is the purposeful course of organizing how your resources will be safeguarded, made due, and appropriated after your passing or in the occasion you become weakened. It incorporates something other than the dispersion of resources — it's about inner harmony for yourself and security for your loved ones.

It includes going with basic choices today to safeguard your friends and family's tomorrow, guaranteeing that your domain is moved to your recipients as easily and proficiently as could really be expected.

Key Instruments of Home Preparation

Wills: The foundation of any domain plan, a will is an authoritative record that determines your desires with respect to the dispersion of your resources and the consideration of any minor youngsters. Without a will, the state concludes these issues, frequently in manners that probably won't line up with your expectations.

Trusts: A trust is a guardian game plan that permits an outsider, or legal administrator, to hold resources for the benefit of a recipient or recipients. Trusts can be utilized for different purposes, for example, staying away from probate, decreasing home expenses, and accommodating the administration of your resources in the event of inadequacy.

Overarching legal authorities: This record awards somebody you trust the position to go with choices for your benefit, would it be advisable for you become unfit to do as such. This can cover monetary, lawful, and medical care choices, guaranteeing that your undertakings are dealt with as per your inclinations.

Medical services Mandates: Otherwise called a living will, this record frames your desires in regards to clinical therapy on the off chance that you become unfit to impart those choices yourself.

Exploring the Intricacies of Bequest Arranging

While bequest arranging can appear to be overwhelming, its intricacy is sensible with the right direction. Talking with legitimate, charge, and monetary experts can give important bits of knowledge and assist with fitting a domain plan that lines up with your interesting conditions and objectives. An interaction requires insightful thought, however the inner serenity and security it offers you and your friends and family are incomprehensible.

The Effect of Home Anticipating Your Inheritance

Bequest arranging is in excess of a monetary methodology; it's an impression of your qualities, your affection, and your heritage. It permits you to offer a significant expression about what your identity and makes the biggest difference to you. By assuming command over this cycle, you guarantee that your heritage is safeguarded by your desires, offering direction and backing to your friends and family even in your nonappearance.

The Fundamental Job of Home Preparation

As we close this part on home preparation, recall that the choices you make today about your bequest are among the main in forming the eventual fate of your abundance and the prosperity of your friends and family. Bequest arranging is a urgent part of abundance the executives, for the rich as well as for any individual who wishes to settle on a conscious decision about their heritage. In the fabulous plan of your monetary excursion, it addresses the smart zenith of a daily routine very much experienced, guaranteeing that your heritage perseveres and thrives in the possession of those you value.

Safeguarding Your Resources

In the odyssey of abundance creation and the executives, shielding the resources you've perseveringly amassed against potential dangers is a urgent section. Resource security, a system as significant as gathering itself, includes organizing your monetary undertakings to prepare for unexpected cases, claims, and lenders. This part unfurls the methodologies and legitimate systems intended to safeguard your abundance, guaranteeing that your monetary inheritance stays in one piece and keeps on prospering for a long time into the future.

Figuring out Resource Assurance

Resource assurance is the craft of putting your abundance past the span of likely loan bosses and defendants while complying with the stated aim of the law. It's about precautionary preparation — organizing your resources in a manner that, should a lawful case emerge, your abundance is safeguarded and protected. This doesn't suggest sidestepping real commitments or concealing resources; rather, it's about shrewd, lawful procedures that safeguard your monetary prosperity.

Techniques for Viable Resource Insurance

Viable resource security starts with understanding the instruments and designs accessible:

Proprietorship Designs: What you own your resources can fundamentally mean for their weakness. Holding resources through trusts, restricted obligation organizations (LLCs), and different substances can give layers of insurance, isolating privately invested money from business dangers and safeguarding resources from individual lawful difficulties.

Property Exceptions: Numerous purviews offer insurances for your main living place under estate regulations, which can safeguard a part, while perhaps not all, of your home's estimation from banks.

Retirement Records: Government and state regulations frequently give significant assurances to retirement accounts like IRAs and 401(k)s, perceiving the significance of getting one's retirement against monetary commotion.

Homegrown and Seaward Trusts: Trusts, whether homegrown or seaward, can be a viable device in resource security. These game plans can put resources out of direct possession, under the stewardship of a legal administrator, with limitations custom-made to your insurance needs and monetary objectives.

Exploring Lawful and Moral Contemplations

Resource security arranging is nuanced, requiring cautious route of lawful and moral contemplations. The line between legal assurance and fake movement — moving resources for dodge loan bosses — can be fine. Early and proactive preparation, in a perfect world before any cases emerge, is fundamental. Talking with legitimate experts work in resource security and bequest arranging guarantees that systems are both compelling and consistent with the law.

The Job of Resource Assurance in Abundance The executives

Integrating resource assurance procedures into your abundance the board plan isn't a demonstration of suspicion yet reasonability. Life's capriciousness, combined with the quarrelsome idea of our general public, makes it basic to find intentional ways to protect one's abundance. Past its nearby advantages, resource insurance arranging builds up the construction of your home arrangement, guaranteeing that your resources are circulated by your desires, unaffected by outside claims.

Sustaining Your Monetary Heritage

As we finish up this investigation of resource insurance, obviously shielding your abundance isn't just a guarded methodology yet a basic part of mindful abundance the board. By carrying out viable resource insurance measures, you secure your own monetary future as well as the heritage you wish to abandon. In the great story of your monetary excursion, let resource security act as the fortification inside which your abundance can develop, protected from the tempests, fit to be passed down as a demonstration of your prescience and stewardship.

Altruism and Inheritance Building

As the story of abundance advances from collection and security to its last parts, the concentrate frequently moves towards the enduring effect one wishes to abandon. Charity arises for of offering back as well as an incredible asset for heritage building, installing your qualities and vision into the structure holding the system together. This part investigates the significant connection among altruism and abundance the executives, outlining how vital giving can improve your heritage while encouraging positive change on the planet.

The Embodiment of Altruism in Abundance The board

Altruism, at its heart, is the outflow of one's qualities and responsibilities through the committed assignment of assets to causes and associations that reverberate with those convictions. It rises above simple monetary commitments, epitomizing a comprehensive way to deal with abundance that thinks about its more extensive cultural effects. For some, generosity is the most private and significant part of their heritage, offering a method for sustaining their qualities and impact far past their lifetime.

Key Giving for Greatest Effect

To guarantee that charitable endeavors are all around as significant as could really be expected, key arranging is fundamental:

Recognize Your Charitable Objectives: Explain what you desire to accomplish with your giving. Whether it's supporting training, propelling clinical examination, or safeguarding the climate, having clear objectives can direct your altruistic exercises.

Research and Select Causes: An expected level of effort is key in choosing associations that line up with your qualities and have a demonstrated history of viability and straightforwardness.

Think about Different Giving Vehicles: From direct gifts to laying out a beneficent trust or establishment, different vehicles can expand the effect of your commitments while furnishing tax cuts and lining up with your bequest arranging targets.

Connect with Relatives: Generosity can be a strong method for joining a family around shared values. Including relatives in humanitarian choices can assist with imparting those qualities in people in the future, guaranteeing the coherence of your heritage.

Generosity as A component of Bequest Arranging

Integrating magnanimous surrendering to your bequest plan can essentially improve the heritage you abandon. Inheritances, altruistic trusts, and establishments not just guarantee that your generous objectives are met however can likewise diminish home assessments, guaranteeing a greater amount of your abundance goes to your expected recipients and causes. Vital generosity takes into consideration a smart dispersion of your riches, mirroring your life's qualities and needs.

The Advantages of Giving

Past the monetary and tax reductions, charity enhances the provider's life, offering satisfaction and a feeling of direction. It interfaces people to their networks and to the more extensive human experience, giving a point of view that abundance alone can't offer. Generosity is an interest in a superior future, one where the abundance one has collected serves individual interests as well as everyone's benefit.

Decision: Making a Heritage Through Magnanimity

As this part shuts, the job of generosity in abundance the executives and heritage building is clear. It addresses a significant chance to engrave your qualities on the world, guaranteeing that your abundance fills a need past the collection of resources. In the excursion of abundance the executives, generosity remains as the zenith of living an existence of importance. Through essential giving, you can make an inheritance that rises above material riches, one that adds to the improvement of society and moves people in the future to convey forward your obligation to having an effect.

Chapter 5: Mastering the Wealth Mindset

Persistent Learning and Development

The excursion toward dominating the abundance outlook starts with a basic standard: the obligation to ceaseless learning and self-awareness. In the powerful scene of growing a strong financial foundation, the landscape is steadily changing, set apart by the development of business sectors, innovations, and methodologies. To explore this scene effectively, one should embrace the ethos of a long lasting student, continually looking for information, improving abilities, and adjusting to new real factors. This section is devoted to the quest for scholarly and self-improvement as the foundation of monetary thriving.

Embracing a Development Outlook

At the core of consistent learning lies the development outlook, a confidence in the potential for key self-improvement. Dissimilar to a proper outlook, which sees capacities as static, a development mentality blossoms with challenge and sees disappointment not as proof of unintelligence but rather as a gladdening springboard for development and for extending existing capacities. In the domain of riches, taking on this outlook implies seeing each monetary choice, each venture, and, surprisingly, every misfortune as a valuable chance to learn and turn out to be more capable at exploring the intricacies of monetary development.

Systems for Long lasting Learning

The way to keeping a development mentality and encouraging consistent learning includes a few key systems:

Remain Informed: Routinely draw in with monetary news, market patterns, and financial conjectures. This doesn't mean responding to each variance yet fostering an educated point of view on long haul patterns and open doors.

Look for Instructive Open doors: Whether through proper training, online courses, studios, or books, grow your insight on monetary subjects, speculation techniques, and financial standards. The objective is to construct an expansive and profound comprehension that illuminates more intelligent monetary choices.

Embrace New Innovations: The monetary world is progressively advanced, with advances like blockchain and computerized reasoning reshaping markets and potential open doors. Keeping up to date with these progressions can open up new roads for growing long term financial stability.

Reflect and Audit: Consistently evaluate your monetary choices and the results they yield. This intelligent practice assists with incorporating examples learned and refine methodologies pushing ahead.

The Effect of Persistent Learning on Establishing long term financial stability

The obligation to nonstop learning and development significantly affects growing a substantial financial foundation. It not just outfits you with the information and abilities expected to settle on informed choices yet in addition cultivates strength against the unavoidable vulnerabilities of the monetary world. Additionally, it opens up new skylines for abundance creation, permitting you to perceive and take advantage of chances that others could ignore.

Developing the Abundance Mentality Through Learning

As we close this investigation of persistent learning and development, recall that the excursion to abundance isn't a run however a long distance race. It requests steadiness, interest, and an immovable obligation to self-awareness. By embracing the standards of deep rooted learning and the development mentality, you furnish yourself with the most amazing assets for monetary achievement: information and versatility. In the amazing account of growing a substantial financial foundation, let consistent learning be the directing light that drives you to flourishing, satisfaction, and the dominance of the abundance outlook.

Systems administration and Mentorship

In the multifaceted dance of abundance creation, the means you take are many times directed by the insight and encounters of the people who have traveled before you. The way to monetary achievement is seldom trampled alone; it is cleared with the connections, associations, and experiences gathered from an organization of guides and friends. This part dives into the extraordinary influence of systems administration and mentorship in dominating the abundance attitude, featuring how these connections can sling your monetary excursion forward.

The Force of Association

Organizing, in its embodiment, is tied in with building a trap of connections that proposition backing, counsel, and open doors. It's the trading of thoughts, the flash of motivation, and the way to open doors that could somehow stay shut. With regards to establishing a strong financial foundation, your organization can be a wellspring of venture guidance, business valuable open doors, and basic experiences into market patterns and techniques. About encircling yourself with people challenge you, push you towards greatness, and enlighten ways you probably won't have seen.

Finding and Developing Mentorship

Mentorship takes the idea of systems administration above and beyond, offering an immediate line to customized direction and intelligence. A tutor can be a mentor, an aide, and a sounding board — an individual who has explored the intricacies of growing long term financial stability and will share their insight to assist you with staying away from entanglements and exploit open doors. Finding a tutor includes recognizing somebody whose accomplishments line up with your objectives and whose exhortation you regard and worth. Developing this relationship is about something other than learning; it's tied in with building trust, exhibiting responsibility, and being available to criticism.

Procedures for Viable Systems administration and Mentorship

Be Proactive: Go to industry meetings, workshops, and systems administration occasions. Join online gatherings and virtual entertainment bunches connected with establishing financial stability and speculation.

Offer Worth: Systems administration is a two-way road. Consider what you can propose to your organization and tutors, whether it's your own bits of knowledge, abilities, or backing.

Remain Locked in: Stay in contact with your contacts through standard updates, questions, or sharing articles and data of common interest. Commitment keeps the relationship alive and complementary.

Be Open and Inquisitive: Move toward each discussion as an amazing chance to learn. Pose smart inquiries, listen effectively, and be available to new viewpoints and thoughts.

The Effect on Growing a strong financial foundation

The effect of a powerful organization and solid mentorship on establishing a strong financial foundation couldn't possibly be more significant. These connections can speed up your expectation to learn and adapt, open up new venture roads, and furnish you with an emotionally supportive network during both prosperous times and unavoidable misfortunes. They can likewise upgrade your standing, giving you believability and a stage from which to send off or develop your establishing long term financial stability tries.

The Aggregate Excursion to Abundance

As we wrap up this investigation of systems administration and mentorship, recollect that the excursion to abundance is definitely not a singular undertaking yet an aggregate excursion. It's a journey best explored with the insight of guides and the help of an organization that shares your yearnings. In the tremendous expanse of growing a strong financial foundation, let these connections be your compass and your anchor, directing you toward your monetary objectives and then some. Systems administration and mentorship are methodologies as well as interests in your most important resource — yourself.

Defeating Deterrents and Mishaps

The excursion to abundance is certainly not a straight way however a street set apart by slopes and valleys, victories, and difficulties. The genuine proportion of an abundance developer isn't just in that frame of mind of resources however in the versatility to defeat the unavoidable difficulties that emerge. This section is committed to the specialty of exploring monetary snags, changing mishaps into venturing stones towards more prominent monetary strength and intelligence.

The Certainty of Monetary Difficulties

No excursion to abundance is without its difficulties. Market vacillations, speculation misfortunes, business disappointments, and startling life altering situations are only a couple of the obstacles that can influence your monetary advancement. These minutes test your purpose, your systems, and your capacity to adjust. Perceiving that misfortunes are not the end but rather a piece of the cycle is significant in fostering the flexibility expected to move ahead.

Building Flexibility Through Difficulties

Flexibility even with monetary difficulties is a developed expertise, brought into the world from an outlook that sees deterrents as any open doors for development and learning. This viewpoint permits you to move toward misfortunes with interest instead of dread, inquiring, "What can this show me?" as opposed to, "For what reason is this occurrence to me?" It's tied in with keeping a drawn out vision, understanding that the way to abundance is long distance race, not a run, and that steadiness is vital.

Techniques for Conquering Monetary Snags

Keep up with Point of view: Keep misfortunes in setting. They are in many cases transitory and can be overwhelmed with time and vital activity. Recollect your drawn out objectives and the purposes for your growing a substantial financial foundation venture.

Gain for a fact: Examine what prompted the misfortune. What can be realized? How might you change your systems to keep away from comparable impediments later on or to relieve their effect?

Remain Adaptable: adjust your arrangements. Adaptability is a vital quality in exploring monetary scenes, permitting you to turn procedures because of evolving conditions.

Look for Help: Rest on your organization and coaches. They can offer counsel, share their own encounters of conquering difficulties, and give the consolation expected to endure.

The Job of Mishaps in Establishing long term financial stability

As opposed to diminishing your excursion, misfortunes assume an essential part in establishing financial stability. They are the manufacture where your monetary intuition is tried and reinforced. Every snag defeat adds a layer of strength and insight, preparing you better for future difficulties. They show you risk the board, the significance of enhancement, and the benefit of having a strong monetary establishment.

Embracing the Excursion, Hindrances what not

As this section closes, obviously difficulties are not just hindrances however vital pieces of the growing a substantial financial foundation venture. They give significant examples, test your systems, and at last, add to a more significant comprehension of monetary administration. By embracing these difficulties with strength, gaining from them, and remaining focused on your objectives, you change potential hindrances into impetuses for development and achievement. In the rich embroidery of your monetary excursion, let the strings of persistence and flexibility weave an account of strength, driving you to the abundance and life you imagine.

Abundance and Prosperity

In the terrific quest for monetary overflow, it's memorable's fundamental that abundance is nevertheless one part of a rich and satisfying life. This section enlightens the profound interconnection among abundance and prosperity, stressing that genuine flourishing envelops monetary accomplishment as well as private satisfaction, wellbeing, and satisfaction. About finding some kind of harmony takes into consideration both the collection of riches and the development of a daily routine worth experiencing.

Understanding the Abundance Prosperity Nexus

Abundance and prosperity are inseparably connected, each affecting the other in significant ways. Monetary security can give an establishment to prosperity, offering genuine serenity, opportunity, and the resources to seek after one's interests and interests. On the other hand, individual prosperity upgrades one's capacity to accomplish monetary objectives, driven by a feeling of direction, energy, and the strength to confront life's difficulties.

Offsetting Monetary Objectives with Life Objectives

The quest for abundance shouldn't come to the detriment of wellbeing, connections, or individual satisfaction. Accomplishing balance includes laying out monetary objectives that line up with your qualities and life objectives, guaranteeing that your establishing financial stability endeavors improve as opposed to take away from your general personal satisfaction. About settling on informed decisions reflect the main thing to you, considering an agreeable mix of monetary achievement and individual satisfaction.

Systems for Improving Prosperity Close by Abundance

Focus on Wellbeing: Your physical and emotional well-being are your most prominent resources. Put resources into them as tirelessly as you do in your monetary portfolio, through standard activity, a fair eating routine, and care rehearses.

Develop Connections: Rich connections are a foundation of prosperity. Sustain your associations with family, companions, and local area, perceiving that these bonds are significant wellsprings of help, delight, and satisfaction.

Seek after Interests: Permit space in your life for exercises that give you pleasure and fulfillment past work and monetary undertakings. Whether it's specialty, music, travel, or a side interest, these pursuits improve your life and add to a balanced feeling of riches.

Practice Appreciation: Developing a mentality of appreciation can change your view of riches and achievement. Routinely recognizing what you have, instead of focusing on what you need, encourages satisfaction and a feeling of overflow that rises above monetary measures.

The Effect of Prosperity on Monetary Achievement

An even life, where prosperity and abundance commonly support one another, makes a temperate cycle. A condition of prosperity upgrades your mental capabilities, imagination, and critical thinking skills, straightforwardly helping your monetary undertakings. All the while, monetary strength upholds your prosperity by lessening pressure and empowering you to put resources into your wellbeing, connections, and interests.

Decision: Creating a Tradition of Genuine Riches

As we close this investigation of riches and prosperity, let us reclassify being really affluent. Abundance isn't simply a proportion of monetary resources yet a comprehensive condition of overflow that envelops wellbeing, bliss, connections, and individual satisfaction. In your excursion toward monetary achievement, make sure to mesh prosperity into the texture of your life, making a tradition of genuine abundance that rises above financial measures and improves each part of your reality. In the great story of your life, let the sections of riches and prosperity be permanently connected, each enhancing the other, directing you toward an existence of complete success.

Conclusion: Bringing It All Together

Summing up Key Examples Learned

As we stand at the edge of this excursion's end, it's fundamental to think about the journey we've embraced together. Through the parts of this book, we've explored the complex yet compensating scene of establishing financial stability, uncovering the insider facts that can prompt monetary autonomy and success. This end serves as a snapshot of reflection as well as a signal, directing you to return to the center illustrations that structure the bedrock of an effective growing a strong financial foundation technique.

The Underpinnings of Riches

We started our process by figuring out the significance of a strong groundwork — planning, crisis reserves, obligation the executives, and putting resources into oneself. These underlying advances are vital, making way for monetary security and development. Like the foundations of a powerful oak, a solid groundwork upholds the far reaching development on the way, guaranteeing versatility against the erratic tempests of life.

The Force of Effective financial planning

Investigating the domains of effective financial planning, from the securities exchange to land and then some, we revealed the instruments through which abundance isn't simply saved however duplicated. The standards of accumulating funds, risk the board, and broadening were enlightened, displaying how educated, key venture choices can dramatically expand your monetary assets over the long haul.

High level Systems for Abundance Upgrade

Wandering further, we dove into cutting edge techniques that refine and amplify the growing long term financial stability process. Charge productivity, the making of recurring sources of income, and the pioneering soul were featured as roads through which abundance can be both sped up and defended, it is vigorous and feasible to guarantee that your monetary development.

Safeguarding Your Riches and Heritage

Recognizing that abundance isn't just to be amassed however safeguarded and passed on, we investigated the basic areas of protection, home preparation, and magnanimity. These parts guarantee that your abundance serves your lifetime's objectives as well as those of people in the future, implanting your qualities and vision into the actual texture of your heritage.

The Abundance Outlook

Woven all through each technique, each knowledge, was the fundamental string of the abundance mentality — a point of view that embraces nonstop learning, strength despite difficulties, and the harmony among riches and prosperity. This mentality is the compass that directs each choice, each activity towards the skyline of independence from the rat race.

Truth be told

As we distil the embodiment of these parts into key examples, recollect that establishing financial stability is both a craftsmanship and a science. It requests persistence, steadiness, and an eagerness to learn and adjust. The standards framed in this book are your devices, your guide, and your compass. With them, you are exceptional to explore the excursion ahead, transforming dreams of monetary freedom into the real world.

As we finish up this part, let these examples be a light in the dimness, enlightening the way to a future where abundance isn't simply a chance, yet a sureness. With each step taken, with each example applied, you move nearer to opening the genuine capability of your monetary excursion.

Following stages: Significant Objectives and Arranging

With the scene of establishing a strong financial foundation investigated and the key illustrations scratched to us, the following part of your process entices — a section not written in these pages, but rather on the material of your life. The information you've gained is a money box of potential, however its actual worth is acknowledged exclusively through activity. This part is devoted to changing experiences into significant stages, making an arrangement that drives you towards your monetary desires.

Laying out Significant Monetary Objectives

Start by taking shape your monetary objectives. These ought to be explicit, quantifiable, feasible, important, and time-bound (Savvy). Whether it's accomplishing monetary freedom, purchasing a home, putting something aside for retirement, or subsidizing instruction, every objective ought to mirror your most profound qualities and goals. Get these objectives on paper, for recorded as a hard copy, they move from the domain of thought to the plane of activity.

Making a Customized Growing long term financial stability Plan

Equipped with your objectives, the subsequent stage is to draft a guide — a customized growing long term financial stability plan that frames the techniques and activities expected to transform your monetary dreams into the real world. This plan ought to incorporate:

Planning and Cost Administration: Laying out a spending plan that lines up with your monetary objectives, focusing on reserve funds and venture.

Venture System: Concluding the amount of your assets will be dispensed to various speculation vehicles, in light of your gamble resilience and time skyline.

Risk The executives and Security: Consolidating protection and home wanting to shield your resources and inheritance.

Nonstop Learning and Development: Focusing on continuous training to refine your methodologies and adjust to changing monetary scenes.

Carrying out Your Arrangement

With your arrangement close by, the center movements to execution. This requires discipline, responsibility, and ordinary checking and acclimation to remain lined up with your objectives. Separate your arrangement into sensible activities, setting momentary achievements that act as venturing stones to your bigger goals. Commend these achievements as you contact them, permitting them to fuel your inspiration and responsibility.

Looking for Proficient Direction

Think about enrolling the help of monetary experts — counselors, organizers, and coaches — who can give ability, responsibility, and point of view. Their direction can be significant in exploring complex monetary choices and keeping on track towards your objectives.

The Way ahead

As you stand on the slope of activity, recall that the excursion to abundance is iterative, a progression of steps taken consistently, each structure on the last. Your customized establishing a strong financial foundation plan isn't permanently established; it is a living record, developing as you develop and as your conditions change. The genuine proportion of achievement lies in arriving at your monetary objective as well as in the development experienced en route.

Embrace this next section earnestly and transparency, prepared to apply the examples learned and leave on the functional strides towards your monetary future. Your excursion to abundance is extraordinarily yours, loaded up with potential open doors for learning, development, and accomplishment. With each forward-moving step, you draw nearer to understanding your monetary dreams, making a tradition of thriving and satisfaction.

The Excursion Ahead: Determination and Versatility

As we divert the pages from wanting to activity, it becomes clear that the excursion ahead is both promising and testing. Setting out on this way with an abundance of information and a diagram close by is only the start. The genuine pith of establishing financial stability lies in the actual excursion — the strength to persist through moves and the versatility to explore the always changing monetary scenes. This part is devoted to embracing the excursion, with all its promising and less promising times, as you step towards your monetary objectives.

Embracing the Long distance race, Not the Run

Establishing financial stability is a long distance race, a drawn out try that requires tolerance, ingenuity, and the guts to keep with it. The way is seldom direct, set apart rather by patterns of progress and times of stagnation or even relapse. These changes are not marks of disappointment but rather are characteristic for the course of development. Embrace them with persistence, understanding that each step, whether forward or in reverse, is a piece of your excursion towards monetary freedom.

The Urgent Job of Versatility

The monetary world is dynamic, impacted by financial cycles, market unpredictability, and arising valuable open doors. Outcome in this climate requests versatility — the ability to reconsider your systems, make informed changes, and turn when fundamental. This adaptability permits you to exploit new open doors, moderate dangers, and keep advancing towards your objectives even as conditions develop.

Gaining from Mishaps

Mishaps are inescapable, however they are likewise important learning open doors. Each challenge presents an opportunity to extend your comprehension, refine your systems, and fortify your strength. Move toward difficulties with an outlook of interest and transparency, inquiring, "What can this show me?" as opposed to harping on the mistake. By separating examples from these encounters, you transform hindrances into impetuses for development and progression.

Remaining Focused on Persistent Improvement

The excursion to abundance is one of nonstop improvement, a promise to gaining from the two victories and disappointments. Routinely audit your monetary arrangement, praise the achievements accomplished, and consider the examples learned. Remain informed about monetary patterns and developments, and be ready to adjust your techniques accordingly. This obligation to development guarantees that your way to deal with establishing long term financial stability stays important and compelling, regardless of what's in store.

Outlining Your Course with Certainty

As we think about the excursion ahead, let constancy and versatility be your directing stars. They are the characteristics that will support you through the difficulties, engage you to jump all over chances, and empower you to explore the intricacies of the monetary world with certainty. Keep in mind, the way to abundance is as much about the excursion for what it's worth about the objective. It's an excursion set apart by self-improvement, learning, and the fulfillment of chasing after your monetary dreams.

Embrace the street ahead with an open heart and an immovable soul, prepared to confront the difficulties and embrace the open doors that lie on the way to monetary freedom. Your process is remarkable, an impression of your yearnings, assurance, and the insight acquired with each forward-moving step. With determination and flexibility as your mates, you are exceptional to graph a course towards a future overflowing with thriving and satisfaction.

Last Uplifting statements

As we wind down this excursion through the scenes of abundance creation, it's essential to stop and ponder the ground we've navigated together. The way to monetary autonomy is as much about the actual excursion for what it's worth about the objective. A way requests flexibility, devotion, and a resolute obligation to your vision. This last segment is planned to act as a reference point of motivation, a wellspring of inspiration to drive you forward as you keep on exploring the intricacies of creating and supporting financial stability.

The Groundbreaking Force of Devotion

The quest for abundance is a demonstration of the groundbreaking force of devotion. Each step taken, each technique carried out, and each impediment defeat is an impression of your obligation to accomplishing independence from the rat race. This devotion is the fuel that drives progress, changing desires into substantial real factors. Allow it to be an update that with resolute responsibility, the objectives that once appeared to be far off can be brought reachable.

Embracing the Abundance Outlook

At the center of this excursion is the abundance outlook — a viewpoint that perspectives challenges as any open doors, mishaps as illustrations, and development as a continuous interaction. This mentality is your compass, directing your choices, molding your techniques, and affecting your way ahead. Embrace it completely, for it is the establishment whereupon enduring abundance is assembled. It enables you to see past the prompt, to imagine a future characterized by overflow and flourishing.

The Excursion Proceeds

Keep in mind, the excursion to abundance doesn't end with the end of this book. It's a consistent journey, one that develops with each new experience, understanding, and accomplishment. Remain inquisitive, stay adaptable, and continue to push the limits of what you accept is conceivable. The way to monetary freedom is cleared with steadiness, learning, and the boldness to wander into the unexplored world.

A Splitting Idea

As you stand on the limit of what's straightaway, outfitted with information, techniques, and an abundance mentality, pause for a minute to recognize how far you've come. The excursion ahead is yours to shape, loaded up with boundless potential and unfathomable open doors. Let the illustrations learned light your direction, and may your commitment to your monetary objectives rouse the accomplishment of abundance as well as the acknowledgment of a daily existence wealthy in reason, satisfaction, and delight.

All things considered, let these last encouraging statements act as a directing light, enlightening your way toward independence from the rat race. The excursion to abundance is perhaps of the most significant experience you can set out on — an undertaking that challenges you, develops you, and at last, rewards you in manners unimaginable. Continue onward with certainty, versatility, and an open heart, for what's to come is brilliant with the commitment of the abundance you're bound to make.